MotorSports

ATV Racing

by Bill McAuliffe

Consultant:
Roger Ansel
Manager of Amateur Competition
American Motorcyclist Association

CAPSTONE
HIGH/LOW BOOKS
an imprint of Capstone Press
Mankato, Minnesota

Capstone High/Low Books are published by Capstone Press
818 North Willow Street • Mankato, MN 56001
http://www.capstone-press.com

Library of Congress Cataloging-in-Publication Data
McAuliffe, Bill.
    ATV racing/by Bill McAuliffe.
        p. cm.—(Motorsports)
    Includes bibliographical references (p. 46) and index.
    Summary: Introduces the history, different types of races, safety concerns, and
other aspects of all terrain vehicle racing.
    ISBN 0-7368-0024-7
    1. All terrain vehicle racing—Juvenile literature. [1. All terrain vehicle racing.]
I. Title. II. Series.
GV1037.M32 1999
796.72—dc21   98-7055
                                                          CIP
                                                          AC

The author would like to thank Craig Chapman of "45" Racing for his help in
preparing this text.

Editorial Credits
Michael Fallon, editor; Timothy Halldin, cover designer; Sheri Gosewisch, photo
    researcher

Photo Credits
Janine Pestel, 4, 24, 27, 28, 43
John Pellan, 6, 14, 18, 20, 22, 32, 34, 37, 38, 40
Photo Finish, cover
Photo Network/Nancy Hoyt Belcher, 16
Victory Sports, 9, 30
Visuals Unlimited/Deneve Feigh Bunde, 10; Mark E. Gibson, 13

Table of Contents

Chapter 1

ATVs

ATVs are lightweight, open vehicles with balloon tires. The balloon tires can travel over many surfaces because they have heavy tread. The tires can absorb shocks from rough surfaces.

ATV stands for All-Terrain Vehicle. Terrain is the surface of the land. ATVs can travel on rough land, including deserts and mountains.

ATVs can travel on surfaces that many other vehicles cannot. People drive ATVs on hills, rocks, and sand. ATVs also can travel through shallow water and mud.

ATVs have handlebars like those on motorcycles. Drivers use handlebars to steer ATVs. Throttle and brake controls are on ATV handlebars. ATV drivers can easily reach these controls to speed up or stop their TVs.

People buy more ATVs than motorcycles each year. People use ATVs to help with their

ATVs can travel on hills and through mud.

work. ATVs can pull trailers and haul heavy objects on farms and ranches. Many people also buy ATVs to race.

ATV Racing

ATV racing is a motorsport. Motorsport racers drive vehicles on tracks or courses. ATV racing is similar to motorcycle racing. But ATVs have four tires and do not go as fast as motorcycles. The top speed for an ATV is about 80 miles (129 kilometers) per hour. Motorcycles can go up to 180 miles (290 kilometers) per hour.

ATV racers enjoy challenges. They race side by side on narrow tracks. ATV racers drive through mud pits and over obstacles. They slide through turns at high speeds.

ATV racing is very dangerous. ATV racers receive training and know how to use their vehicles. They wear protective safety equipment and follow safety rules. ATV manufacturers recommend that all new riders take ATV training classes.

ATV racers often race side by side on narrow tracks.

ATV Racers

Almost anyone can race ATVs. Both adults and children race ATVs. Boys and girls can start racing when they are six years old. All racers must wear safety gear and know safety rules before they can race.

ATV racers belong to different racing classes. Classes of racers race only against each other. Race organizers base racing classes on age and rider ability. ATV racers who are around the same age and have similar abilities race against each other. The racers in each class use ATVs with similar engines and parts.

Both adults and children race ATVs.

Chapter 2

ATV Racing History

A Canadian company made the first ATVs during the 1950s. These early ATVs had six wheels. People used these ATVs to travel on rough terrain.

Farmers and ranchers used ATVs to herd cattle and sheep. The ATVs were easy to drive off-road. The balloon tires could go through mud and over obstacles without getting stuck.

Three-Wheel ATVs

Companies made the first three-wheel ATVs during the 1970s. The first three-wheel ATV was the Honda ATC90. Farmers and ranchers found three-wheel ATVs as useful as six-wheel models.

People thought that the three-wheel ATVs were fun to ride. Many people bought three-wheel ATVs during the 1970s and 1980s. They often rode them on trails and beaches.

Early ATVs had six wheels.

But three-wheel ATVs were dangerous. They rolled over easily. Thousands of riders were hurt in accidents. Safety officials wanted companies to stop making three-wheel ATVs. In 1987, the companies that produced three-wheel ATVs agreed to stop making them.

Four-Wheel ATVs

Suzuki made the first four-wheel ATV in 1983. Four other large manufacturers also began to make four-wheel ATVs. They were Kawasaki, Yamaha, Honda, and Polaris. By 1987, companies were selling thousands of four-wheel ATVs. Companies switched to making only four-wheelers.

All ATV manufacturers made special ATV models just for racing. Racing ATVs had powerful engines and strong suspension systems. Suspension systems have springs and shock absorbers that attach to wheels. Suspension systems protect racers from the bumps on rough terrain.

In the 1980s, racing ATVs were no longer profitable to make. So ATV manufacturers

Three-wheel ATVs were dangerous and rolled over easily.

The AMA sanctions more than 1,100 ATV racing events each year.

stopped making them. Many top racers today use ATVs that are more than 10 years old. The most popular racing model is the 1989 Honda Four-Trax 250R.

The First ATV Races

The Pine Lake Summer National was one of the first ATV races in North America. This race took place in 1970 in Ashtabula, Ohio. The competitors raced six-wheel ATVs.

The Pine Lake Summer National still takes place. ATV racers now ride four-wheel ATVs rather than six-wheelers. People from all over the world gather to watch the best ATV racers compete in this event.

Race organizations sanctioned more ATV races during the 1980s. To sanction means to approve an event and make it official. In 1982, the American Motorcyclist Association (AMA) sanctioned its first ATV race. The AMA now sanctions more than 1,100 ATV racing events each year. Up to 19 different racing classes can compete in the races. The racing season lasts from January to December. Racers receive trophies and money when they win races.

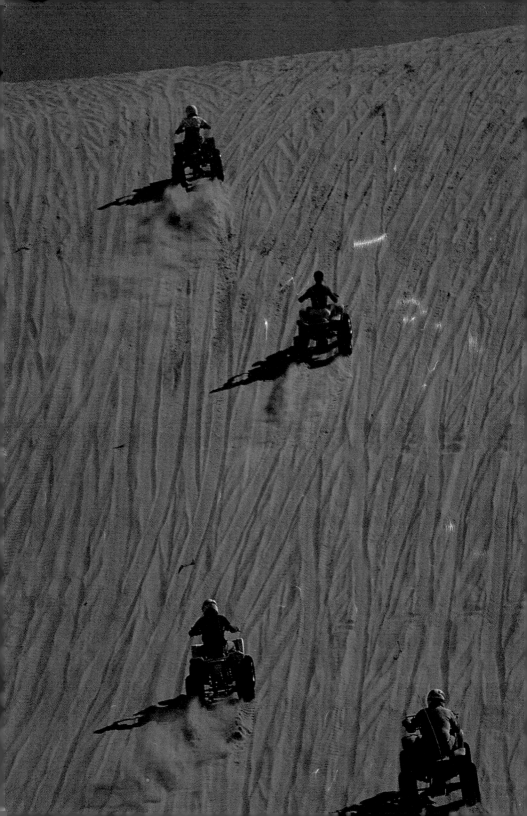

Chapter 3

ATV Parts

Many racing ATVs are modified stock vehicles. ATV racers make changes to vehicle parts that come directly from manufacturers. Racers alter the engines, suspension systems, or other parts on their ATVs. They try to make their ATVs more powerful and easier to handle.

ATV engines can be either two-wheel drive or four-wheel drive. Two-wheel-drive ATVs have engines that send power to the back wheels. Four-wheel-drive ATVs send power to all four wheels. Racers can change some ATVs from two-wheel to four-wheel drive by pressing buttons on the vehicles.

Four-wheel drive is necessary when tracks or courses are steep. ATVs climb hills better when powered by four wheels. Two-wheel drive is useful when ATVs must go around sharp

Racers use ATVs with four-wheel drive to climb hills.

ATVs have balloon tires that protect racers from shocks.

curves. Two-wheel-drive ATVs turn more easily than four-wheel-drive ATVs.

Important ATV Parts

Important ATV parts include the engine and the suspension system. The engine powers a sprocket that turns the wheels. A sprocket is a wheel with teeth that fit into the holes of a chain. The sprocket turns the chain, and the chain drives the wheels. ATV racers need strong sprockets and chains that will not break during races.

Balloon tires also are important on ATVs. They cover the wheels and protect the ATV racer from shocks. Tires have tread on them to help racers stay on rough roads. Axles hold the wheels in place on ATVs.

ATV racers use exhaust pipes to increase engine power. Exhaust pipes carry away waste gases produced by engines. Gas tanks hold gasoline to power ATV engines. Most ATV gas tanks hold three to four gallons (11.4 to 15.1 liters) of gasoline. Gas tank protectors cover the gas tanks. They keep rocks or flying objects from puncturing gas tanks.

ATVs have throttles and brake controls on their handlebars. Drivers press throttle controls to make their ATVs speed up. They press brake controls to slow down ATVs.

The Cost of ATV Racing

ATV racing costs thousands of dollars. Good racing ATVs cost about as much as some cars.

Many ATV racers own two or more of the best racing ATVs. ATV racers also need trucks and trailers to carry their ATVs.

ATV racers spend extra money on parts and repairs during a racing season. They must regularly replace the drive chain and sprocket. Racers replace their tires often. Several sets of tires can wear out during a race.

Manufacturers improve parts for ATVs each year. They use lighter metals in the new parts. They design stronger frames and more powerful engines. ATV racers often look for new parts that will make their ATVs run better and faster. But these improved parts can double or triple the cost of the ATVs.

Manufacturers design strong frames for ATVs.

Handlebars

Balloon tires

Axle

Gas tank protector

Engine

Chapter 4

ATV Tracks and Courses

There are two main kinds of ATV racing. One kind takes place on race tracks. Dirt tracks are oval shaped and have banked curves and straightaways. Straightaways are the flat and straight parts of tracks. Motocross tracks have sharp curves, hills, jumps, and irregular terrain. Large walls surround the tracks and separate racers from the spectators who watch races.

Race organizers build race tracks at fairgrounds or in arenas. An arena is an oval structure for sporting events. Spectators sit in rows of seats that surround the arenas. Most dirt tracks are at fairgrounds. Most motocross tracks are in arenas.

The other kind of ATV racing takes place on race courses. Race courses travel through open terrain. ATV racers travel on the path toward a

One kind of ATV racing takes place on race courses through open terrain.

finish line. Most race courses are long and pass through many types of terrain. They have many curves but return to where they begin.

ATV racers often crash on race courses. Race organizers sometimes place hay bales in risky areas such as sharp curves. The hay bales protect riders from harm if they run their vehicles off the courses.

Racing on Tracks

The most popular kind of ATV race tracks are motocross tracks. Spectators enjoy watching ATV racers go over jumps and around sharp curves. These tracks are one-half to one and one-half miles (.8 to 2.4 kilometers) long.

Another kind of ATV race track is the dirt track. These tracks are one-eighth to one-half mile (201 to 805 meters) long. Race organizers often build small dirt hills called whoops into the tracks. Whoops cause ATVs to lift into the air during races.

A third kind of race track is the ice track. Race organizers build these tracks during

Whoops are small dirt hills that cause the ATVs to lift into the air during races.

winter in the northern United States and Canada. Race organizers build the tracks on frozen lakes. The race tracks usually are oval and flat.

ATV racers must prepare their vehicles before they race on ice tracks. They alter their engines to run well in cold air. They then put studded tires on their ATVs. Studded tires have small metal spikes or screws that grip the ice.

ATV racers speed through mud in cross-country races.

The tires keep the ATVs from sliding during ice races.

Races on tracks usually are only a few laps long and last just a few minutes. ATV racers must go as fast as possible to beat other racers. Racers could lose a race if they make even one mistake.

Racing on Courses

One kind of race course is the cross-country race course. Cross-country race courses have narrow paths. The paths go over jumps, through woods, and across fields. ATV racers speed through streams and mud. The tires of their ATVs spin on gravel. Racers try to dodge fallen trees and climb steep hills.

ATV racers race single file on cross-country race courses. The paths are too narrow for more than one racer at a time. Race officials record the time it takes for each racer to finish the course. The racer with the fastest time wins the race.

ATV racers must be careful on cross-country race courses. Racers often cannot see far ahead on the paths. Cross-country race courses have many sharp curves. Trees and other large obstacles on the courses block the view.

Another kind of cross-country race course is the hare scramble race course. Race organizers build these courses away from large cities and towns. The beginning of the paths are wide enough for up to 50 ATV racers at one time.

ATV racers jockey for the lead during hare scramble races.

Then the paths narrow. ATV racers jockey for the lead. They try to get good racing positions in the group of racers before the paths narrow. Hare scramble races usually last an hour or more.

Famous Courses
The Baja 500 and the Baja 1000 are the most famous cross-country race courses. Races have

taken place on these courses since 1967. The Baja 500 takes place in June, and the Baja 1000 takes place in November. The Baja 500 course is about 500 miles (805 kilometers) long. The Baja 1000 course is about 1,000 miles (1,609 kilometers) long.

The Baja race courses wind through the Baja California Desert in Mexico. ATV racers, off-road truck racers, and motorcycle racers compete in the two races. The race courses are different each year. Race organizers try to make the courses as challenging as possible.

ATV racers compete in the Baja 500 in teams. Each racer in a team must travel a set distance and then give the vehicle to another racer. In 1997, the winning ATV team covered the course in 12 hours and 56 minutes.

Another famous ATV cross-country course is in Hurricane Mills, Tennessee. ATV racers compete there for the AMA Grand National Cross-Country Championships. Adults and children both take part in these races.

Chapter 5

ATV Races

ATV racers prepare for races. Racers must make many quick starts, stops, and turns in their ATVs during races. Racers check the engines, brakes, suspension systems, and handlebars on their ATVs before racing. These parts must work well for racers to win races.

ATV racers usually arrive four or more hours before a race. Racers often walk the race tracks to gather important information. They find out if any objects or obstacles may cause problems during a race. Racers also look for loose soil or mud. These places can be slippery. After walking the tracks, they can make changes to their engines, suspension systems, or other parts if necessary.

ATV racers examine the whole race track or course if they can. But cross-country courses

ATV racers must prepare for their races.

Up to 20 ATV racers wait at the starting line to begin a motorcross track race.

are usually too long for them to walk. Racers can learn about cross-country courses by asking race officials or other racers who have raced on the courses.

ATV racers can make a plan for the race if they know the track or course. Racers want to learn where there are turns, whoops, or straightaways. Racers can decide to accelerate in straightaways and slow down in curves.

Practice Laps

ATV racers sometimes take practice laps on race tracks before races. Racers usually take their first laps very slowly. This allows them to feel what it is like to drive on the tracks. Then ATV racers take a few laps at full speed to test their vehicles.

ATV racers attend drivers' meetings before races start. Racers and race officials discuss the racing rules. ATV racers also talk to each other and exchange racing tips during the meetings.

Two Kinds of ATV Races

Motocross races start with up to 20 ATV racers. All the racers line up at the starting line at the same time. Once the race starts, the lead racers change places at every corner or on every jump.

Many racers push their ATVs too hard on the motocross tracks. Their ATVs may break down and they cannot finish the races. Racers sometimes must jump over whoops on the dirt tracks. But it is better for racers to keep their ATVs on the ground. ATV racers cannot accelerate their ATVs if they are in the air.

During races, racers must be able to think and act quickly for a long time. ATV racers often crash into obstacles on the cross-country courses. Their ATVs may become stuck in mud. ATVs also may break down.

Up to 100 ATV racers begin cross-country races. Racers try to gain a good lead early in the race. The racers often keep the lead for many hours in order to win races.

ATV racers cannot accelerate their ATVs if they are in the air.

Chapter 6

ATV Racing Safety

Only experienced riders should try ATV racing. ATV race courses and tracks have many dangerous jumps and curves. Inexperienced ATV riders can hurt themselves if they are not careful and safe while racing.

Lawmakers no longer require ATV riders to take safety classes. But most safety experts recommend that beginning ATV riders learn safety rules and drive slowly. The experts say ATV riders should avoid taking jumps and riding on loose soil and steep hills.

ATV manufacturers offer basic riding safety classes to vehicle owners. Manufacturers also recommend that ATV riders wear safety gear.

Safety Gear
Safety gear can protect all ATV users. Helmets are the most important piece of safety gear.

Safety gear can protect ATV riders and racers.

ATV racers must often jump and steer their heavy ATVs.

Full-face helmets are the best kind of helmets. Helmets should fit closely and comfortably over racers' heads. ATV racers should wear goggles or face shields to protect their eyes.

Full sets of protective clothing help ATV racers stay safe. Jackets made of leather protect the chests and backs of the racers. ATV racers also wear pants with pads to protect their legs.

ATV users can wear additional gear for further protection. Off-road style gloves protect hands. Motorcycle boots protect shins and feet. ATV racers wear plastic chest protectors and shoulder pads under their jackets. These pads protect racers' backs and chests from injury during a crash.

Safety Laws

In 1989, the U.S. Government passed a law to protect ATV riders. The law set certain limits on four-wheel ATV use.

According to the law, ATV riders must be at least six years old. Riders between the ages of six and 12 must use ATVs with small engines. ATV riders between the ages of 12 and 16 must use ATVs with medium-sized engines.

Fitness

ATV racing can be a test of strength and stamina. Stamina is a racer's ability to drive for a long time. Racers often must jump and steer their heavy ATVs. They must shift themselves on their seats to keep their balance. Tired racers can make mistakes and hurt themselves or other racers.

Top racers stay in shape for ATV racing. They lift weights and run. They eat healthy foods and do not drink alcohol or take drugs. Most ATV racers compete in other racing sports. Many race mountain bikes. Others ski or run.

ATV racers enjoy the challenge and thrill of ATV racing. ATV racers carefully follow the rules of ATV racing. They wear safety gear to protect themselves so they can always race. ATV racers exercise so they race better. They hope one day to become champion ATV racers.

ATV racers hope one day to become champions.

Words to Know

accelerate (ak-SEL-uh-rate)—to speed up

axle (AK-suhl)—a rod that connects to the center of a wheel and holds the wheel in place

four-wheel drive (FOR-WEEL DRIVE)—a system that transfers engine power to all four wheels of a vehicle

jockey (JOK-ee)—to try to gain the best racing position in a group of racers

obstacle (OB-stuh-kuhl)—something that hinders easy forward progress

sanction (SANGK-shuhn)—to approve an event and make it official

shock absorber (SHAWK ab-SORB-uhr)—a device on a vehicle that lessens the shock of driving on rough surfaces

stock vehicle (STOK VEE-uh-kuhl)—a vehicle with parts that come directly from a manufacturer; mechanics often alter the parts on a stock vehicle.

studded tire (STUHD-id TEYE-ur)—a tire that has small metal spikes that grip ice

suspension system (suh-SPEN-shuhn SISS-tuhm)—a system of springs and shock absorbers on a vehicle

terrain (tuh-RAYN)—the surface of the land

two-wheel drive (TOO-WEEL DRIVE)—a system that transfers engine power to the back wheels of a vehicle

whoop (WOOP)—a small dirt hill on a race track

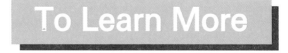

To Learn More

ATV Rider Course Handbook. New York: ATV Safety Institute, 1994.

McKenna, A.T. *Off Road Racing.* Fast Tracks. Edina, Minn.: Abdo and Daughters, 1998.

Smith, Jay H. *The Most Rugged All-Terrain Vehicles.* Wheels. Minneapolis: Capstone Press, 1995.

Useful Addresses

American Motorcyclist Association
33 Collegeview Road
Westerville, OH 43081-1484

ATV Magazine
601 Carlson Parkway, Suite 600
Minnetonka, MN 55305

Dirt Wheels **magazine**
P.O. Box 957
Valencia, CA 91380-1910

Internet Sites

The American Motorcyclist Association
http://www.ama-cycle.org/

The ATV Connection
http://www.atving.com/

Index

All-Terrain Vehicle, 5
American Motorcyclist
    Association (AMA), 15, 31
axles, 19

Baja, 30, 31
balloon tires, 5, 11, 19
brake, 5, 19, 33

chain, 18, 19, 21
chest protectors, 41
cross-country, 29, 30, 31, 33,
    34, 36

dirt track, 25, 26

engine, 8, 12, 17, 18, 19, 21,
    27, 33, 41
exhaust pipes, 19

face shields, 40
four-wheel ATVs, 12, 15, 18, 41
four-wheel drive, 17, 18
frames, 21

gas tanks, 19
goggles, 40

handlebars, 5, 19, 33
hare scramble, 29, 30
helmets, 39, 40

ice tracks, 26, 27

manufacturers, 7, 12, 17, 21,
    39
motocross tracks, 25, 26, 35

obstacle, 7, 11, 29, 33, 36

shock absorbers, 12
six-wheel ATVs, 11, 14, 15
spectators, 25, 26
sprocket, 18, 19, 21
studded tires, 27
suspension system, 12, 17, 18,
    33

terrain, 5, 11, 12, 25, 26
three-wheel ATVs, 11, 12
throttle, 5, 19
two-wheel drive, 17, 18

whoops, 26, 34, 35